ROSSETTI'S WOMBAT

JOE NEAL

First published in the United Kingdom in 2018 by The Choir Press

ISBN 978-1-78963-004-6

Printed in size 11 Cambria.
Edited by Harriet Evans.
Portrait of the author by Tommy Clancy.
Cover design by Jacqueline Abromeit.
Cover illustration: Author on Cnicht,
Snowdonia, North Wales.

ALSO BY JOE NEAL

Telling It at a Slant, Pen Press (2013).
ISBN 978 1 78003 664 9

Turn Now the Tide, Choir Press (2014).
ISBN 978 1 909300 73 6

Hear the Colour, Choir Press (2015).
ISBN 978 1 910864 13 5

Still Rise the Sun, Choir Press (2016).
ISBN 978 1 910864 61 6

The Next Blue Note, Choir Press (2017).
ISBN 978 1 911589 07 5

Readings by the author from these poetry collections
can be heard at:

www.joenealtellingitataslant.com
www.turnnowthetide.com
www.hearthecolour.com
www.stillrisethesun.com
www.thenextbluenote.com

La nuit est une femme à barbe.

Brigitte Fontaine

ABOUT THE AUTHOR

Joe Neal was born half-way up a mountain in North Wales. He began his acting career in repertory theatre before attending Nottingham University. He also trained as a journalist, working for the Western Mail (Cardiff), Times, Guardian, Daily Telegraph and Daily Express.

As an actor, he has performed on stage, radio and television in Britain and Ireland. Between acting work Neal writes extensively on the countryside and natural history as well as devoting time to poetry and short stories which he believes should be read aloud – 'even to oneself.'

He writes of life and all its strife and tells it at a slant – sometimes with the delight of a child rolling boulders down a slope. His poems plunder dreams and memories and bend to the natural world. He says, 'Love, I'm afraid, is a constant theme: lost loves, found loves, hoped-for loves, hopeless love. Mostly the last. But as Clint Eastwood says in the character of Dirty Harry, "A man's got to know his limitations."'

A glutton for punishing experiences, he stood twice as an Independent for Parliament in Britain and once in Ireland for the European elections.

His published work has appeared in the Times, Daily Telegraph, Countryman, Waterlog, New Writer, New Society (now defunct), Ireland's Own, Scaldy Detail and numerous poetry magazines. Performed writing includes *Revenge*, *The Reluctant Trombonist*, *Send in the Clown* and *Kites and Catullus*. He has read the poems of Seamus Heaney and John Betjeman on BBC television and Shakespeare and Dylan Thomas on BBC radio. Recently he had 12 of his poems published in the anthology *Dust Motes Dancing in the Sunbeams*.

In 2017 Joe Neal won the Anthony Cronin International Poetry Award and was invited to perform his readings to music at the AberJazz Festival in Wales. In 2018 he won an Arts Council bursary for a reading tour of America. *Rossetti's Wombat* is Neal's sixth collection of poetry and follows the widely acclaimed *The Next Blue Note* (2017), *Still Rise the Sun* (2016), *Hear the Colour* (2015), *Turn Now the Tide* (2014) and *Telling It at a Slant* (2013). All are available through major book stores worldwide and on Amazon. The author has recorded his readings of all six publications.

Neal says his life has been shaped by his childhood in Morfa Bychan, Gwynedd, North Wales and the Roman town of Colchester, Essex, and – more importantly – by time spent in Ireland, where he now lives. He is divorced and a proud grandparent.

CONTENTS

Foreword   xi

WALKING WILD

High Spirits   1
Allegheny Man   2
Assault of the Sea   4
A Branch Too Far   5
Clubbing   6
Stonechat   8
Shadow of Chernobyl   9
Story Board   10
All Things Bright   11
Rossetti's Wombat   12
Walking Wild   14
Still Rise the Sun   15
The Awakening   16
Living Memory   18
Night Watch   19
Broken Dream   20
Dancing Wild   21
Not So Blind   22
Learning Lear   23
That Tears Might Cease   24
Freudian Slip   25
Belfast Blitz, Easter '41   26
Blowing in the Wind   27
Taken   28
Barbican Buffalo   30
Love at First Bite   31

Buried Pleasure   32

Walking on the Wind   34

Blank Canvas   35

Moth Ball   38

Shades of You   40

ON WITH THE MOTLEY

Come Back, Catullus   43

Rubbler Rhys   44

Watchers   47

Water   48

Time to Say Goodnight   49

Tiger on the Doorstep   50

Music of Antrim   51

Into the Gulley   52

Catcher in the Sky   54

Lady Be Better   55

Learning Curve   56

Celyn Valley   58

Of Moth and Man   59

Really Richard   60

To the Manner Born   61

Pipefish   62

Cold Case, 8 AD   64

Cormorant Boy   66

Suck of the Sea   68

Plastic Caryatid   69

Swipsy Cakewalk   70

Onward and Up   72

Changing of the Light   74

For Otto   75

On with the Motley   76

Centurion   77

Tramp-Lean   78

ILL MET BY SUNLIGHT

Fishfall	81
You're Never Alone with a Spider	82
Ode to an Old Rose	84
No Parallax	85
Stars Are Falling Down	86
Gone but Not Forgot	88
Cambodian Smile	89
Crith of a Heron	90
Silver Adder	92
Moontrap	96
Release	97
Haiku Too Far	98
Bye-Bye Blues	99
Breath of Bechet	100
Ragtime Cowboy	102
The Books That Fell on Me	104
Long-Tailed Tit	106
Turn and Turnabout	107
You Again!	108
Off-Beat	109
The Lie Direct	110
An Evening with Courtney Pine	111
Ill Met by Sunlight	112
Passing	114
Mountain Greenery	115
On State Street	116
Oh, Didn't Jelly Roll!	118
Go with the Flow	119
Night Life	120
The Hare That Dipped Its Paws	122
That Pure Thing	123

FOREWORD

What is the poetic voice? Is it as discernible as the inspiration at the root of an idea or a line? Is it cleft by the bifurcation of time into the past and the present, the poet's effort to segue both with a fresh vision or the recollection of something that may or may not have taken place? Is the poetic voice the caryatid supporting the entablature of the poem, or the mere whisper of a bourn ferrying the mystery of its profounder source? Perhaps the poetic voice is a divining rod for the poet dowsing blindfolded on the exhausted parchment of the imagination.

At the very least, the poetic voice is musical, but the tablature behind the lines of the contemporary poem is not trouble-free. It is vibrant and clear-cut, well defined and ringing, but it is by no means unblemished, because a line without the instinct for music cannot be entirely flawless. Or faultless. The poet's faith in the summons to write and the lines and stanzas which follow is not an apodictic assurance that it is as good as it gets.

For the poetic voice is also a separate material in the manufacture of a poem, one of several which must gel, and is difficult to define. And yet, thanks to the engineering marvel that is the cochlea, we can instantly distinguish the voice of any poet whom we have taken the time – and in poetry time is incalculable – to understand. To absorb. To enjoy. It should be a perfectly natural engagement. In colonies of thousands in the southern hemisphere, birds use vocalisations to tell each other apart, and in a murmuration each bird uses scale-free correlation to stay in synch with each other.

We depend more on the acoustic values of the poetic voice than the logical and lexical exigencies of the written line. This, however, only goes so far. For, as Housman noted, 'Poetry is not the thing said, but the way of saying it.' The poetry and the voice of Joe Neal are as distinct as the cuckoo's call in a dawn chorus rippling through a forest, and he achieves this by thinking and writing foremost as an individual. If the poet can see himself as an original, amorphously free to be shaped by the world in which he is contained like Thoreau at Walden, then the poem is nurtured in the invisible smithy with sufficient emotional and spiritual impulses to take a leap into the beyond.

> *With rasping sighs*
> *the breeze-brashed branches*
> *fling their russetness*
> *through churning skies*
> *to crust the ground*
> *with autumn's pall –*
> *a detritus to delight us*
> *in the coughed-out calm*
> *that follows squall;*
> *and then, oh glory be,*
> *the warmth of sunshine*
> *roding through*
> *the now-still stands*
> *of starkled trees –*
> *as, fussed by feet,*
> *the crispiness of leaves*
> *fumes breathed-in air*
> *with bitter nuttiness!*

In 'Walking on the Wind', Joe Neal's Edenvale is Thoreau's Walden, and reading it aloud you can understand how poetry is a very emotional, very quick and very abrupt medium, and that the poet, like Thoreau, is rich in proportion to the number of things which he can afford to let alone. Each of us will have a preference from the torrent of poetry which has emanated from Joe in the past decade, but we cannot deny that present in each communique or despatch from his pen is his indefatigable humanity.

And I have often felt that his nature poems are always a discovery to the reader because so few of us have Joe's vision, his weft of empathy for the physics of beauty, be that a current or a past love, the minutest arachnid or an imperious raptor in the mysterious essence of flight.

The shapely little dipper,
that curtsied constantly,
would never live to see
the hatching of her eggs.

(from 'Watchers')

Subtract the promise of hatchlings and the river is more or less dead. Yet the significance of the loss of the hatchlings is unquantifiable for the scientist or the naturalist, but not for the poet, for whom the forfeiture of life, even in its simplest form, amounts to the loss of motive power, every bit as dramatic as the denudation of a coastline. In Joe's verse I hear the voice of Aldo Leopold: 'Subtract the grouse and the whole thing is dead.'

And when your raw material as a poet is love and nature and memory – the legacy of Joe's Welsh roots, though he qualifies as Irish – you will find in these poems delights and dilemmas, thought out and reflected upon assiduously, and the pleasure of the poet in remembering something that he didn't know he knew.

To spend time in Joe's company is to appreciate his lifelong memory for every epiphany in a long and well-thumbed career: specifically, Joe has an encyclopaedic knowledge of jazz, the vinyl he has collected and the concerts he has attended, and has the armoury of words to do his memory bank justice.

An e-mail from Joe is not the anaemic electronic communication of modern life that it has become: oh no, Joe can write like a hipster evangelist, exuding a Ginsbergian facility for a rat-tat geyser of words. You don't get to write the following lines, which I received from Joe following his successful reading tour of North America earlier this year, without being the acutest of observers:

One of the other highlights of my US visit was seeing a porcupine in New Hampshire as well as getting a distant glimpse of a moose. Other sightings included a garter snake, squirrels, chipmunks, white-tailed deer, black-legged ticks, loons, phoebes, robins (a kind of rubicund thrush), wild black turkeys, kites, buzzards, monarch butterflies, swallowtails and our own white admirals. But no bears, alas.

But I did get stung by poison ivy. The full American experience, in fact, with a diner thrown in. Also spent a night in a wood cabin and sailed in a 'pinky' New England schooner out of Gloucester, Mass, with some fellow passengers from Ohio who seemed scared to talk to me. That's Mid-West Americans for you!

I also visited a firearms store in Kittery, Maine. (Imagine Tesco filled with guns and fishing tackle and staffed by good ol' boys and you'll get the picture.) A friend wanted to purchase a handgun for home protection against intruders. We hit on a snub-nosed .38 to stop the baddest arse. Me? I'd prefer to hit him with the tribrachic stutter of my poem gun – guaranteed to stun!

The self-deprecation, always in evidence, belies his phenomenal achievement as a stylist which I believe is untinctured by mimicry or the superfluous: no poetry is alive which is merely written, measured in syllables or tinselled with stressed vowels or the reverberation of rhyme. Poetry must be charged by the voice of the poet, recognisably so, and Joe's stands out from the tumult, and that is what the poetic voice should do. Joe's labour is to create the form – the poem – which sustains the relationship with the reader. The process for the writing poet is always malleable, but in your hands this collection, Joe's sixth, will settle into itself.

Tom Mooney
July 2018

Tom Mooney is the former executive editor of Ireland's Echo Group of Newspapers, an award-winning author and editor of the poetry anthology Dust Motes Dancing in the Sunbeams. *He now reviews for the* Sunday Times.

WALKING WILD

HIGH SPIRITS

The climb is long and hard
and breath comes in short gasps,
effort clutching at the chest
and tearing at a pounding
heart until the eyes
no longer see beyond
the boots on cliff above;

Then, at last, with aching
legs astride the sunlit
summit rock, I see,
frighteningly,
an elongated image
of myself, shadow
on the mist from cwm below;

Now I understand why
others speak of ghosts
which terrify the bravest
mountaineer – as diffracted
light makes a spectre
of myself with rainbow
halo round a saintly head.

ALLEGHENY MAN

I knocked and heard a screech and razzle-clump
across a wooden floor – and then I saw
him in the open door, half-in, half-out,
sitting in a chair he'd built to spare
his wooden leg while waiting for repair.
Bartle John his name, though no one knew
from whence he came, a mountain man for sure,
with bear to blame for brutal loss of limb;
whiz mechanic, so they said, who walked

with miracles he worked on bits
of old machinery – and strummed the blues on banjo
made from shagbark hickory, with God-knows-what
for strings, and twanged his 'itty-bitty
trickiness', sometimes 'til moon had bled
into the sun and Allegheny hills
had begun to run with colour of the day.
Now he's gone, panning for the stars – but still
they hear his music drifting in the wind

as curled leaves settle on his grotesque
rotting chair, while salamanders crawl
across the hanging door and tawny
crescent butterflies flutter through the roof.
They say old Bartle John sure could play
and sing the saddest song about life's
wrongs he saw so clearly through unmatched

Walking Wild

eyes of brown and blue which understood
alternate sides of neighbours' arguments.

We never really met – yet in the ruins
of his home, I feel I know him well;
his heavy presence lingers there
like a pulsing shimmer in the air,
while mockingbird and phoebe
stay their song – creatures dumb in awe
of spirit lore, listening for that moving
chair to squeal across the hallowed ground
where Allegheny Man once ruled with sound.

ASSAULT OF THE SEA

Lipizzaner waves confront
the pebble strand,
breaking into froth of trot
then beating back again
to part at hissing
isthmus hinterland
in lull of repetition,
dulling soon with tide
to mezzanine of calm
– furtively returning
to crescendo charge
of white brigade, booming
at the shrinking shores
in bright magnificence.

A BRANCH TOO FAR

Wet white crystals clutch at unaccustomed
brightness from the sky in late December
melt of snow – creased now with drag-tail dent
as creature trails its mark in progress
to the tallest tree; then, at keel of naked
larch, a final five-toe digit print
invites an upward glance from me – and there,
its red brush standing higher than the highest
branch, a squirrel tops the forest in exult
of panoramic view and leaps, reaching
at the air, free-fall turning in the wind,
to plummet groundwards with a tiny shriek.

CLUBBING

Bouncer buzzing bright in flicker neon light,
pale blue robot guarding entry to the gate.
It's Eighties Night; forty-something hopefuls
in skinny jeans and bopping boots queue to be
abused for their not-quite-with-it gear.
Women of a certain age in mini-skirts
fend off expected leer with jagged, painted
scowl, deep down yearning for a lover's touch again.
I recognise that 'robot' now: the hardy
stare, the side-turned nose, that balanced stance,

uncomfortable in black DJ
and frilly-fronted shirt and all-too-perfect
dickie bow clipped tight to bulging neck.
Those fists, hanging big beyond the cuff,
bring back remembered roars of caterwauling
crowd as he bounced about the ring gloving
glimmer out of groggy, grunting men.
The door is open now, changing colours
of the light splashing puddles on the pavement,
first a purple, then a ghoulish green,

as Billy Joel replaces Richie's
'All Night Long' with 'Uptown Girl' and distracted
dancers jump the fizz of frenzy pop
on this our disco-driven night – echoes
of a past when brash music filled a gap

and hardship sat it out against the beaten wall.
We get the look, and then the nod. He lets us in.
The dream is deafening. The bounce is back.
KC and the Sunshine Band start to sing:
'Give It Up' is lost on us – we're too far gone.

STONECHAT

Pebble clink from up a tree
strikes a chord of memory
– look up, you'll see a squat
fat bird with twitching tail
perform its air of mystery;

A flash of white, a dark
capped head and thrust of rufous
chest – a tiny stonechat seeks
asylum in the warbler wood,
ignored by other birds;

Challenging the sky, it towers
towards familiar sun,
dropping now and then, regaining
height in prelude to its
haunting song – double notes

first clear and sharp, then deeper,
throaty, resonating
pure again – lonely bird
without a mate, relishing
its own identity;

It sings the loudest of them all
– robin, lark and thrush –
cadenzas drifting to the ground
in language they don't understand:
a little chat, out of habitat.

SHADOW OF CHERNOBYL

The Pripyat river
gurgles like a Geiger
now as death flows
past a mute and mirthless
carousel of fun;

Stillness mocks Big Dipper,
crucified by caesium
against a poisoned sky
and deadly isotopes
of 239 plutonium;

Radioactive fission
power of four hundred
atom bombs blew gales
as far as mountains
where I climbed in Wales;

And sheep that feed on grass
that grows on slopes
contaminated
by Chernobyl's blast still
register a ghostly click.

STORY BOARD

At ten to one
the billboard blocks the sun
and shadows hide
her printed breasts
in afternoon opprobrium.

Strident, trident
cacti sprong the sky;
sombrero at the tilt
is order of the day
as cicadas sharpen up their symphony.

Desert dust begins
to roll, obliterating shape
of waking rattlesnake;
a limping man looms
to fill the scene – and cut! It's all a dream.

Sometimes I'm roused
before the snake has struck,
before the stranger's cry of pain;
other times I see the naked girl
more starkly lit and yearn to drink her Coke.

ALL THINGS BRIGHT

The band took up the stand
and blew against the rain;
mining men, spick and span
in uniform of black and white,
brought 'Deep Harmony'
to the coal pit head
as thunder rolled
across the mountainside
with eerie muffle boom
– brass chords counting down
the lightning flash to bang;
in that diorama of light,
'Cwm Rhondda' and 'Jerusalem'
brimmed hymning hearts
– and a male voice choir
sang of all things bright
like children had before
they died in Aberfan.

*On Friday, October 21st, 1966, a sliding colliery spoil-
tip buried Pantglas Junior School in Aberfan, killing
116 children and 28 adults from the South Wales
mining village.*

ROSSETTI'S WOMBAT

Top the Wombat slumbered in his basket,
set strategically as dinner centrepiece
while splendid poets round the table
romanticised about the price of velvet
and rippled lips of maid to Mrs Morris,
painted so lasciviously by her
admiring host, the dainty dashing Dante;

Laughter rose as farty snores escaped
from furry face amongst the pepper pots;
all the way from Aussie habitat
the creature came, shipped in upon a whim
of eccentric, esoteric master,
Pre-Raphaelite who took to toucans too,
paraded in his zooey garden

with strapped-on cowboy hats and spurs to boot
a stray tomcat that didn't see the joke;
but death came soon for lonely animals
paraded to impress a coterie
of bored dysfunctionals of fun.
Dante Gabriel Rossetti, you painted well
without the props of popularity;

Someone should have tugged your beard and told you
that armadillos don't eat almonds,
no matter how much laudanum you used

Walking Wild

to lace the meal of an insectivore
with stuff that killed your wife;
no wonder Top the Wombat whistled
to the entertainment of your guests!

Frolics too for friends in the menagerie
of your Chelsea home as spaced-out
wallabies leaped the light fantastic
while you disinterred your lost Elizabeth,
taking back unpublished poems you'd tucked
into her russet hair, beauty fused
in death – such is the power of opium;

Now we ask: did the mad Pre-Raphaelite
– PR to all his friends – dig up the wombat
too? Down there, in that little cemetery
in London's Cheyne Walk, could it be
that loopy lullabies to drugged-up pets
are still waiting to be read by post
Pre-Raphaelites with atavistic urge?

*With thanks to the dramatis personae of the Pre-Raphaelites who documented those events – painters
William Holman Hunt and John Everett Millais,
sculptor Thomas Woolner, critic John Ruskin and poets
Christina Rossetti and William Morris.*

WALKING WILD

We met along the Dorset Path
and one of us turned back
to continue on together;
we talked awhile of Tyneham Gwyle
and people driven out of cottage
homes in D-Day preparation;

We walked the shell-holed streets,
now an archipelago of trees,
and heard a nightingale
speak to us in piquant song
of villagers long gone,
chased off in games of war;

I remember how your tumbled hair
brushed the contours of my map
and how we laughed as you picked out
the pointy snout of Worbarrow Tout
– and you told me how you'd fallen
for the name of Arish Mell;

We headed there – but first
to Dancing Ledge and White Nothe's
chalky cliffs and smugglers'
Brandy Bay – then doubled back
to Durdle Door, dawdling now
in places not yet contemplated.

STILL RISE THE SUN

Dawn walks the hem of darkness,
emerging as the light
– red lamp waxing wanton
in the district of the day;
but how long will it last,
this warmth that twinks through velvet
in speed of white through time?

Until the shrivel moment
when flares of gas run out
and spectrum's but a spectre
in the past – ghost that haunts
the mourning universe
in cold dry sigh of loneliness?
One day no more to rise the sun?

THE AWAKENING

Hush, savour now the silence
of the white wide-face owl,
surprised by cloud-redempted moon,
while, on ground below, a stealth
of noddle mushrooms nudge
the soil away and discreetly
swell upon themselves,
blending musky sweetness
with the velvet ruffled air;
then hear, more clearly now,
the distant plunge of snigging pike,
parting shoal of sash-striped perch
in hunger plunder under
scintillating surface of the lake.

Nothing sleeps as lizard creeps
from out the rock in search
of moisture lush and chance
of insect sustenance;
even dainty sorrel unfurls
its curling petals, sheltered
by the shudder drift of fern;
soon the geese and duck appear
in straggle arrow flight
towards horizon light

and roosting birds detach themselves
from masking thatch of tree to re-begin
their pattern dance across the sky
– and red replaces silver of the night.

LIVING MEMORY

Where once there skimmed
a scanty stream
with angled trees beside,
there now cleaves through
the greening countryside
a straight black rage of road
that scares all life away;

Gone too the red-brick farm
with tench-filled pond
from whence I once saw
lashing eels slime rain-soaked
grass en route to breeding sea;
now there's only stench of factory
and grim clouds chasing off the sun.

NIGHT WATCH

Am I wrong to want to occupy
the secret places of your mind?
Already you have control of mine!
I confess one night I crouched beside
the bed and watched you in your alpha state;
you wore that frown I see when thinking
I'm not listening – the irk that deepens
when I tell you back each word you said;

And now, with every breath you take,
that scowl etches still more deep – until
I bend to feather-kiss those lips and see
your face relax into a secret grace;
did that little peck edit out the bleakness
of your dream – or were you merely faking it?
If only I could listen to your thoughts
I'd know the answer to my quandary.

BROKEN DREAM

In the darkness of their tumble shack
– crofter's cottage piled with clutter
of a former life – the couple toil
in mutual isolation, reaching
with their eyes at gasping candlelight;

Silence speaks in sadness of an empty
dream as they weave and treadle bolts of tweed
unlikely ever to be sold to rich,
discerning island visitors – not trapped,
like them, in downward shift of circumstance.

DANCING WILD

The tide is out, not a soul about
– save for you and me;
the shelf of rock is hard and smooth,
our boots just right
to dance a jig or tap or Lindy hop
to rhythm of the waves;

So we improvise, splashing
in and out of pools,
disturbing scuttle crabs and popping
seaweed pods
as our steps become hysterical,
giggling in the wind;

And, on Jurassic cliff above,
a nodding donkey
tilts in time to pump out oil
from fossil shales
laid down two hundred million
years before.

NOT SO BLIND

He arrived by car, the blind piano tuner,
and tapped his way to our front door, while his deaf wife
waited in the driving seat; sight and sound, they made
a grand duet – but he didn't need her eyes
to render discord into concord on Dad's Bechstein.

Peeping through the half-closed door, I saw him play a note
and disappear behind the shiny propped-up lid,
plucking at a wire until the jagged sound grew round,
fading then to a soft caress; in sight again,
he'd feel his way back to the stool, stabbing at a key

or playing a chord until he found another
noise his ear could not tolerate; he took so long –
tweaking, twanging, thumping, banging – and the repeated
notes up and down the scale were annoying to the ear;
then suddenly came harmonies so sweet that I closed

my eyes, mesmerised, as he conjured colour
out of black and white; I was perfectly in pitch
with my insighted, sightless friend – and knew he saw
another there: 'That's the sound of music, boy,' he said
towards the door ajar. 'Now fetch your dad to me.'

LEARNING LEAR

It is a part I'd always yearned to play
and each day spend time learning it;
you could say then that I'm a secret Lear,
an untried Lear, a Lear-in-waiting;
but I'd choose my Fool with care for he'd be
sometime part of me; an actor's dream
too far to be the foolish king and the Fool
my own reality; it only takes
an ounce of civet to sweeten man's
imaginings – why, I even sprouted
facial hair to seem as Lear should look
– like the god envisaged as a child,
a very Leary god, all-powerful
yet prone to toxic tantrum, hot lava
rage that fizzles into madcap acts
of epic vandalism, killing those
we love so much and aiding all we hate.

Blow, winds, and crack your cheeks,
for Lear is drawing near!

THAT TEARS MIGHT CEASE

Sadness was a voice he'd not forget:
how it stealthed into his childhood dream
from a room beyond that snuggly bunk!
So empty of all hope, those heaving sobs,
that he was drawn in worried puzzlement
to dare the stairs and tend the tide of tears
a mother wept in desolation.

Years on, he heard those same bleak sounds
when a girl he'd loved discovered
she was not alone in his affection;
this time round there was no consoling arm,
though all the hurt was very much the same;
but life takes hostages and soon
it was his turn to make that sorrow sound.

FREUDIAN SLIP

If Freud had liked music,
would his id have been so odd?
My alter ego tells me, *No,*
get off the couch, you've missed the point;
but even so my unconscious
promptings, libido set aside,
suggest an infantile neurosis
that turns rhythm into hate
and blanks his mind to beauty
as a prelude to escape.

What goes on behind the curtain
before that dance of abreaction?
And cannot music really
be the food of everybody's love
– for a people traumatised?
Freud, if only you had heard
that climactic major chord in C
in Scriabin's *Ecstasy*,
would we be still so all alone
in a world that now lacks mystery?

BELFAST BLITZ, EASTER '41

Her mam was in the Slug and Lettuce
when the fire bombs hit – she told her this
when she was old enough to understand;
the Hop Exchange was gone and seventy
dead in Percy Street – so was the Indian
where her aunty waited at the tables;
but the mam was safe to take a drink
while army men went on the hunt
for wolves and tigers, bears and lions,
fleeing in terror from the blitzed-up zoo.

BLOWING IN THE WIND

On a scale of one to seven
I'm on the slide
– bit like my trombone;
ensemble playing's fine,
tailgate too (you growler)
but solo? – oh no,
you're not quite good enough
to blow the dust;
you're just for show.

It was different once;
while vinyl turned
at thirty-three and a third,
I gigged with music's best
– but no one heard.
They're all dead now,
they were all dead then.

Armstrong, Bechet, Jelly Roll
and Fats – and Kid Ory for duets,
and, in my later phase,
Mingus, Miles and John Coltrane,
but their sounds live on
– jazz that says it all
in notes of black and white
                        – and blue.

TAKEN

Come back, it's time the tide returned
– you cannot reach the other side
before the waters sweep your legs away;

Hand in hand the couple walked
across the bay uncovered by the sea
and heeded not the warning call:
come back before the tide returns;

Beckoned by the castle rock – Harlech
from afar – they walked barefoot through drying
pools and felt the sun-warmed hardness of the sand,
unaware they'd never reach the other side;

The boy who'd shouted after them
followed in pursuit, further than he'd ever
been allowed, and tried to hold them back
before the waters swept their legs away;

Don't go, don't go, he begged in fear
for them – but they failed to see
the danger they were in without
the sight and sound of pounding waves;

In tears the boy ran back alone to safety
of the shore and watched two tiny figures
flee to beat the doom approaching them:
too late, too late – the tide's returned

Walking Wild

– you cannot reach the other side
before the waters sweep your legs away.

Weeks on, their bodies reached the Harlech beach,
but still the fearful boy kept watch all summer long
– lest others follow in their steps.

BARBICAN BUFFALO

Do you remember when,
after a first-night party,
we tapped and danced
the Buffalo along the Tube
platform and bellowed out
our finale song?

And how, at the Barbican,
a station man called Singh
had looked on, startled,
in his smart white turban
while we echoed down
the tunnel – step, step,
tappety step – and imagined
the crowd's applause?

Your forward journey took
you on to New York's
Broadway, mine to West
End theatreland;
but what of Mr Singh?
Does he dream of Bollywood
and dancers on the Circle Line?

All the trains I've caught
since then bring
that moment shunting back;
is it the same for you?

LOVE AT FIRST BITE

You are sitting at the sushi bar
watching food rotate;
your choice, I note, without debate
is chicken udon served with spice,
mine's a dish of that gyoza duck;

I offer you a wedge of it
and you respond with pepper
seasoned squid; no names,
no introductions – just the chewy
contemplation of Japanese cuisine;

We follow up with yakisoba
prawn, then plump for plates
of puffy pumpkin korroke;

Our tastes have intertwined
– this is now a dinner date
and the promise in your smile
is of something more to come!

BURIED PLEASURE

Places mean a lot to us,
and never more so than when
entrancement of a moment
can be shared with someone else;

The spraints I leave to mark
the spot for future co-joined
interest are buried wines
of tasteful vintage quality;

Look, beneath the moss and ferns
of Killincooly, in dappled shade
there lies a Médoc, seasoned
Bordeaux lodged in cleft of rock;

Or join me at Tacumshin
Lake to drink my Muscadet
and watch arctic terns
dip and flake the surface in display;

Carrickbyrne's a charming spot,
so what about a hidden Hock
before you clamber up the hill
past bramble-tangled thorn?

Asti Spumante for airy Inistioge
and for Tintern Abbey a Chablis
– or was it Montrachet? – I forget,
I lost the map where X marked the site;

Walking Wild

Crossfarnogue and Ballynaclash,
Owenduff River and Curraghmore
all have Sancerre stashed down there
to suit their moods of peace;

Rioja at sandy Raven Point
and Alsace Riesling in Fethard-on-Sea;
no ordinary plonk for Sillare Rock,
my favourite Fleurie's laid down there;

And here, in wooded Edenvale,
a white Macon perfectly suits
the trickledown, dickledown
streel of the Sow;

So, if you see me prowling
with my trowel and hear
the clink of drink, you'll know
I'm on another vintage spree;

Do join me then,
and share a toast with me
before discerning worms
can penetrate the cork;

But you cannot bury bottles
in a panoramic sky,
like the rosé-rumpled duvet
swaddling sleepy Enniscorthy;

Instead, fix the gaze or paint
the scene upon your mind
for later telling over wine
or beer in some hostelry of love.

WALKING ON THE WIND

With rasping sighs
the breeze-brashed branches
fling their russetness
through churning skies
to crust the ground
with autumn's pall –
a detritus to delight us
in the coughed-out calm
that follows squall;
and then, oh glory be,
the warmth of sunshine
roding through
the now-still stands
of starkled trees –
as, fussed by feet,
the crispiness of leaves
fumes breathed-in air
with bitter nuttiness!

BLANK CANVAS

The hardest thing, I always think,
is making that first move –
seizing the moment of the mood,
for blank stands the canvas,
yearning for the beat of colour,
that signal of intent.

Imagine you're behind a microphone
and must sing that opening phrase
unrehearsed, or slide
into the trombone blow;
but then you know
it can only be in blue.

So you stand at the crossroads,
palette winking paint
– every wodge represents a GO;
now dare you be a Daniel?
Go on, improvise, extemporise
– oh, just get on with it,
aim the gun and SHOOT.

With that first precision dab
you make your mark, select
your ground – all things
stem from that one shape;
now, burdened with destiny,

that little dot of paint
is a challenge to the pristine
whiteness, urging its response.

But this attack is just too
tentative, too subdued ...
and then you see, in your
mind's eye, how other artists
painted with such relish;
how then to emulate the lunge
and plunge of Pollock?
Or slash and parry of other
paintbrush swordsmen?

No. Re-begin with swash and buckle gusto,
shouting now: Take that, you snivelling
canvas. Splash into the turpentine,
wallop into the globs of paint,
frantic flourish on the palette
and then fierce stabs of colour
on the wretched, cowering surface.

The spell is broken,
sickly inhibitions roll away;
you grab the biggest brush
and fall upon the easel
with a blind and berserk fury.

Breathless, you stop to view
the carnival of carnage,
to inspect your desecration;
but now a new, more subtle
force has come upon you:

Walking Wild

This won't do, you say.
Change gear. Select another mood.

More serene. Call it indigo.
Picasso would have approved!
So you slop and prod with bristle brush
and shapes take form –
like burnt sienna blushings
you may see in the fresh-cut
section of a tree.

Then your mind begins to wander,
straying into strange places – like:

> *Why do women hug cushions?*
> *I tried once and felt a fool,*
> *so I placed it behind*
> *my head and slept instead.*

Now, the moving, moody brush
has fashioned you a smiling face,
a young girl, you think
– your Mona Lisa, who just knows
that bilateral symmetry is SO BORING!

MOTH BALL

Shunning mask of darkness,
star-bright seething shapes
congregate on moonwash
white of wall: Eyed Hawk
partners plum-brown Lappet
in the moth ball of the night;

Tiger burning cream and red
and black accompanies
an Elephant in pink –
fresh from willowherb
and woodbine lick;

Convolvulus cavorts
with carmine Cinnabar,
proboscis sucking sweet
from bindweed's
counter-clockwise creep;

Next comes ghostly Vapourer
with rare Blue Underwing,
drifting on the scent of thyme
then resting side by side
on lichen-covered rock;

Joining them in beam
of bright: Lackey, Eggar,

Walking Wild

Magpie, Footman, Fox
and Goat – until the air
is all a mist of wings,
kaleidoscope afloat;

So let us set it all to music
– Moonlight Serenade
for insect *son et lumière*,
but soon the butterflies
will come as lunar lightness
fades to morning sun;

First Peacock flirts
with Tortoiseshell,
then Red Admirals choose
flowers of buddleia,
scorning Cabbage White
who partners dodge of shadow,
unaware she's all alone.

SHADES OF YOU

At night when you're away from me
I start to paint your memory:
how you seemed to me, in pastel
shades, last day we met.

Sometimes, acrylic's best
– or stark black lines of ink
to plot the jagged mood I'm in.

You see, when I paint or draw,
we're all the one,
a passion marled and intricate,
born on my palette.

And if my sable brush should dally
on your face – or other regions
of your naked form – I feel
your presence too,
for that's the art of love.

ON WITH THE
MOTLEY

COME BACK, CATULLUS

So, Catullus, you wrote
a lot of near-the-knuckle
stuff, couched in rhythms
that defied analysis
– chasing your Lesbia
with the urgent relish
of iambic and trochaic time.

Sex to you was the measure
of your effervescent age,
all of two thousand years ago;
that will to shock
still seems so relevant,
as does your odyssey
through the grossness
of Roman high society
– whilst civil wars
and caesars seized the day.

Now it is we who endure
such tribulation,
with equal need
for desperate diversion;
so, Catullus, grab us
by the short 'n' curlies,
tell us how to conjugate
the truth – as patrician
politicians defaecate
their circuses of lies.

RUBBLER RHYS

Into the house
the hardy man came
from the field;
no word was said
as he stomped
his mud boots
on the slate-slatted floor,
while his wife
fussed over his tea.

No word was said
as he tore at the bread
with his split spaded nails,
clay-grouted
from scrawping potatoes
all rain-sodden day.

No word was said,
not even a sound,
as she watched her man eat,
her thoughts not of pity –
or even disgust,
but of pride and of dread
for his new job next week
was under the ground.

On with the Motley

No word was said
but she knew that
each day she'd pray
for her mining man's
safe return.

Then, as he supped
at his tea,
their eyes challenged
and held in a love
that would meld
them as one.

'Don't worry, my dove,
I'll always be coming
back home to thee.'

***

Three wavering notes
the bugler blew
and the quarrymen
ran from the cave;
the clogwyn walls
repeated the sound
with the surge
of an echoing wave;
and then a great hush
as the rockmen
readied the charge.

The first blast came
with a rumbling thump

and a tumble of slate
as the heart of the mountain
broke with a quake.

When the dust cloud
rolled from the cavern's
wide maw, one fearful
shout was joined
by a roar:
'Where's Rhys?' they cried.
'We saw him before.'

His body was found,
crushed by the slate;
poor Rubbler Rhys
had been too deaf
to hear from time
at the Front
with world war
in his ear.

> *Gareth 'Rubbler' Rhys*
> *Blaenau Ffestiniog*
> *North Wales*
> *1894–1926*

WATCHERS

Mizzen tail held high, the distant
watcher side-stepped on the branch,
prating all the while, drawing
other magpies to its grandstand view.

Soon there were two – but not for joy
with what they had in mind;
sorrow beckoned to the object
of their gorgon gaze.

For on the broken bridge below,
another bird of black and white
flitted through the morning mist,
bearing shags of moss
to chosen nesting site.

The shapely little dipper,
that curtsied constantly,
would never live to see
the hatching of her eggs.

WATER

Sun-soaked soil blisters bright
then crumbles dun as dust
to wait the puddle-thump
of rain that makes a broth,
browning mud to leach
to reaching root of tree,
anointing seed (fresh-born)
to cotyledon green,
wetting too through
pastureland that tilts
towards a gloating sea.

TIME TO SAY GOODNIGHT

London's wartime blitz that killed Al Bowlly
while reading Tom Mix cowboy books in bed
also did for Snakehips Johnson, flattened
in mid-song by undiscerning bomb.
In death there's no discrimination –
though two crooners taken in a raid
makes you wonder just what number Adolf had
in mind for doughty Brits chanting 'tootle-pip'
to Doodle Blip in pause before the bang.

The one that took poor Johnson stopped short
of Tuxedo Junction in his Love For Last Time set.
Oh Johnny, How You Can Love, he sang
in Café de Paris cabaret
as death came through the roof to join the band.
Bowlly had recorded Time To Say Goodnight
before his direct hit; distraught fans, Dancing
In The Dark, said he'd a Date With An Angel
and Hitler'd meet the devil in the end.

TIGER ON THE DOORSTEP

Being with you was such ecstasy,
as if all tenses had become
the one – passions pulling
silken threads of past,
present and of future
into a triptych of ourselves.

But then a blackened quirk
of chance carried you away
and I was left bereft
of that better part of me,

Until the night I saw,
lighting up my doorstep,
the incandescent colours
of a garden tiger moth –
reminder that your beauty
had never left this earth.

MUSIC OF ANTRIM

Bring her the harps
and hammer dulcimers
of dreaming County Antrim;
let music be the swirl
of mist enfolding
memory with time.

Still, from a continent away,
she sees blue-knuckled hills
cuffed by lush of trees –
and puffs of dirty gunsmoke cloud
curling in the breeze.

But for those plucked
sounds, she would be blind.

INTO THE GULLEY

Led on by screaming officer
with stick and pistol gun,
we did the chicken run –
knowing bullets couldn't
carry *all* the names we had.

Pals beside me paid the debt
but I charged on, drawn
by thrust of my own bayonet
– and I was through.

Shrapnel Gulley, they called
the valley – Snipers' Alley,
I'd have said!
We were the ANZACs
– 9th Battalion, A Company,
to be precise; sergeant me,
from Wales – not an Oz.

I just went there for a job
– but this war came up
and I volunteered to do my bit;
wearing glasses made no differ,
they said to me, you'll carry
a rifle, cobber, like the rest of 'em.

On with the Motley

Gallipoli's an awful place,
the Dardanelles all the hells
in one; I was seasick
when we landed, so much noise
from whiz-bang shells and gun.

No time to think, just move on;
kill the Turks or they'll kill you.
Whose king? Whose country?
I don't know. Are you safe at home?
Are the Turks in Sydney yet?
Or up my North Wales mountain
– chasing sheep?

The telegram you're reading
now says *Missing Believed Dead*.
No one knows where I rest my head.
Just another body in the Gulley;
the war that didn't end all wars.
Think of me when you buy that poppy
– it's the colour of our blood.

*James Muncaster Lovett, 303, Sgt. Infantry. 9th
Battalion, South Australian Regiment. Missing believed
killed. Last seen escorting prisoners, Shrapnel Gulley,
Dardanelles, April 25th 1915. Gallipoli Peninsula.
Slaughter of the Innocents. RIP.*

CATCHER IN THE SKY

Word is, brother, you've moved on
– gone to another place,
left no forwarding address,
but I know otherwise: you see,
you're still with me in my mind;
I just have to close my eyes.

Others say they saw you
looking peaceful
after all those tests,
and later you were carried
off, quite ornately,
as the compliments
kept coming – like cake
to a cricket commentary box.

But you're there,
out in the field
at deep backward square
leg, waiting for the catch.

LADY BE BETTER

It is the primacy of pulsing beat
that draws me to the Basie band,
how saxman Lester Young's dry harmony
stands alone against the tidal wave
of riffs in unison laid down
by well-honed brass: Lady Be Good
could not be better in their hands,
nor of their successors playing today.
But as for me, I sometimes think I am
that guy the song's about, alone once more,
misunderstood; oh, Lady Be Good
again to me and we can spin that tune
with Lester serenading us on sax!

LEARNING CURVE

The sparrow hawk, fierce
of orange eye, barred
feathers rufous, blue and white,
stood sedate, centre stage,
on a branch above the barn.

Beside her dithered
two young ones, stage right;
below, as 'twere on apron front,
a rabbit munched and sniffed
and hopped a bit
– but never once looked up.

The scene was set, missing,
though, the buskined hero
belting out his tragic monologue.

Now watch on.

With sideways sliding glide,
the hook-beaked mother hawk
hangs above the furry innocent,
yellow legs and claws thrust out
– and shows the way to pounce.

Children follow suit, clumsily,
and then back off, mewing
like the cats they definitely are not.

On with the Motley

Three times they perform this act
and then fly off together,
hunting lesson dusted, done.

Exit rabbit, stage left,
not even chased.
Life's a game. This time ...

CELYN VALLEY

Sometimes nature's flooding rains can claim
a whole community and life will never
be the same again;
but for man to drown a thriving village
deliberately – not with bouncing bomb
in time of war, but when church is full
of song and people talk and get along –
that's beyond the pale.

And yet it happened to a peaceful place
called Capel Celyn just fifty years ago;
eight hundred acres
of productive land, twelve farms, a chapel,
school and post office – and livelihoods
of people too – all to fill a reservoir
for strangers far away.

Gone are homes with names like Tynybont
and Dol and Penbryn Fawr – and a farm
where early Quakers
met in glow-worm light of valley night –
and a Welsh-speaking village which kept its
culture in the face of changing time;
now tombstone names swim wet in double death
decreed by Albion.

*In memory of a North Wales village, its history and its
people, sacrificed to supply the water needs of another
nation. Never again – byth eto.*

OF MOTH AND MAN

The red dot creeping slow against the cliff
was smaller than the caterpillar
munching mighty at my feet;

Perspective lent the stripey horn-tailed
creature green giant status as it ate
into the leaves of clinging mountain plant;

With scope I watched the figure grope a ledge
defying the placing of his feet – knowing
grub will make a moth, he himself a man.

REALLY RICHARD

– lines written following the discovery of the bones of
Richard III.

Car parks usurping history,
Wars of Roses and lost causes;
old bones of a warrior king,
kudos in cathedral places
– battleground for teeming tourists;
no horse now, no Yorkist
crowndom in Elizabethan time
– but buried life rehabilitated,
for Richard was a kindly man,
much put upon by little princes
and the words of William S
– a story of identity
with a spinal twist.

TO THE MANNER BORN

The style they'd chosen
for the decor of the room
was a nod to neo-classical baroque
– though the daughter of the house,
who'd offered me the student job
of painting it, was proving
far less willing than the nymphs
that Bacchus chased across the ceiling.

For soon I was to know
that if you didn't have
that touch of class
enjoyed by privilege,
you needn't chance your arm;
still I had the work and earned
my crust to supplement the grant
I'd lost in a bluffing poker game.

Two lessons learned: stick
to who and what you know
and keep your place where you belong,
and so I write and act
and play the fool a bit
with my trombone; I wonder what
she did with her exotic life
– not that Bacchus gives a stuff!

PIPEFISH

How you must have twitched
and flailed upon the rock
as searing sun bailed
moisture from your
dwindling tidal strand;

How your pouting mouth
must have sucked
and puffed to push
and siphon water through
those fluttering
filaments of gill;

How you must have fought
to stay upright in your
eelgrass habitat as the sea
that held you seeped away;

And how you were left
to lie in wait for your
horizontal, gasping death.

Thus I found you,
high and dry, beyond
the succour of the waves,
still so elegant
in your elongated form;

And now you adorn
my mantel shelf,
hard and brittle,
grey as dust,
a little life force spent.

COLD CASE, 8 AD

When Ovid did a bunk
to what is now Romania
he carried with him
guilt he dared not share with history
– a dirty deed and words
in verse that went too far.

'My poem, my mistake'
was all he'd ever say
to explain the shame of exile
from Augustus Caesar,
once the poet's friend.

Now we cannot help but try
to guess the game he played,
high stakes that cramped his stately
style and beat him into peasanthood.

A fling with wife of royalty
and art of love he put in rhyme
to her would prompt a fall
from grace not out of character.

But could it be a hit and run
with chariot and words
he wrote to cover his offence
while under influence of drink?

On with the Motley

For there was a crime the senate
voted to investigate
in AD Year of Eight,
the time of Ovid's exodus
– cold case that fits with history
when a rival, lesser poet
had life's verse reversed
with brutal suddenness.

CORMORANT BOY

Somewhere, in Ireland, there stands a rock ...

No words he ever heard
or spoke – the awkward,
gangly boy, taunted
for his hearing loss.

He spends the days away
from bruising human company,
finding kinship
with the kinder ways of nature.

In silent, solitary walks
he senses all about him
and sees and feels
what noisy people miss.

One day he happens on a cave
behind a waterfall and wonders
at the gauze of mist that shuts
him from the world he left.

Ahead he scrapes his way
through tunnels in the rock
until a light before
reveals a shelf above the sea.

Now he sits there, staring
at the sun – darkened silhouette

among cormorants who bring fish
and leave them at his feet.

For centuries, they say,
he's kept a vigil from the ledge;
buachaíll cailleach dhubh
they call the rock.

I'll take you there
if you dare to brave
the waterfall like
that lonely cormorant boy.

And if you listen,
you can hear
the speaking waves
as they well against the cliff:

Buachaíll cailleach dhubh,
buachaíll cailleach dhubh ...

SUCK OF THE SEA

Lashes of rock cut through the froth waves,
kinks in the current to hazard the brave
who hanker for herrings that shoal in the sea

ta-rarara-ree, ta-rarara-ree

About the ship comes in haul of the net,
slap to the swell as keel drags on weed,
tilting the decks in suck to and fro

ta-rarara-ro, ta-rarara-ro

Then, with a snap, bow breaks free of the pull
and gouges a path through dull of the trough
to shudder to safety, the hulk and her crew

ta-rarara-roo, ta-rarara-roo

PLASTIC CARYATID

Skills absorbed in execution of a sketch
of Athens' beautiful Erechtheion
match spills of ink, artist's spraint consumed
by ancient marble step – student tourist's
blemish on gamboge stone of Parthenon,
there for the next millennium or two.

Finished drawing then was parcelled up and sent
with love, and Hellenic stamp, to a girl
called Jen, crafted from afar (Caryatid
third from left) in Winsor Newton tint
that brimmed with shining black affection.

But it didn't last: I'd moved on – like always,
drawn by thoughts of greener grass behind the hill
– until, years on with all my options gone,
I too now languish like a plastic
memory in a case of glass, alone
and looked at but no longer stirring hearts.

*Sadly, I own to spilling Indian ink on the steps of the
Parthenon; the original Caryatids, maidens holding up
the roof, were later moved to the Acropolis museum to
escape being eaten by the acid air. Plastic replicas now
take the strain.*

SWIPSY CAKEWALK

When you rang I was washing
my trombone;
in seventh position and slide
right out, it just fits the bath.

Suds in the bell,
then rinse with gel,
rub down and dry,
then polish it well.

Time for a tune;
what will it be? Careless Love
– played in C?

What's that you say?
Either me or my trombone?
Let's see:
okay, you go. I'll blow.

So now I'm Nobody's Sweetheart;
didn't we have A Fine Romance?
All right, I promise: There'll Be
Some Changes Made.

I see, you want All Of Me;
must I really play Bye Bye Blues?
You used to love Swipsy Cakewalk,
and what about One O'Clock Jump?

On with the Motley

Okay, I know, I'm just
a Big Butter And Egg Man.
You know what, you're just
a Hard Hearted Hannah!

Why don't you Come On
And Stomp, Stomp, Stomp?
Surely Our Love
Is Here To Stay?

Must I Sit Right Down
And Write Myself A Letter?
Am I just a Stranger
On The Shore?

You say you've
had too much
of Blues My Naughty
Sweety Gives To Me.

But isn't that
the Glory Of Love?
Now I Don't Get Around
Much Anymore.

ONWARD AND UP

Parting at the estuary
was such bleak sorrow
for you and me –
dirged by eisteddfodau
of scoter, grebe and guillemot
and clarinetting oyster bird.

Turning to the mightiness
of rising rock for strength
to carry on alone,
I hunched into the wind
and yomped away the misery,
ouzel-piped aboard
a mountain floating
in the drift of mist.

Following the white-bibbed
darkling thrush (dodging
screes and crags
in jouncing furtiveness),
I pressed past snow-stilled
frozen mops of scrub
– and forgot we'd ever met.

Arriving, ouzel-led
before the rising jut,
I found a cave

to shiver through
my nightfall purgatory.

Taking soundings then
to meet the sun
(feet in thousands,
on and up – ETA
the dawning day),
I saw my life a climb
apart from yours,
ready to be drawn astray.

*The ring ouzel is a bird of the mountain; its piping call
and flight of hide-and-seek among the rocks can lead
you on and up.*

CHANGING OF THE LIGHT

The sun is changing colour, perceptions
are evolving like ripples in the air,
ultra-ultra wavelengths elongating
beauty beyond the wit of physicists.

Listen, you can hear the shades of yellow
murmur in the brightness of the light,
morphing into orange then relaxing
to a red you've never seen before.

Just you wait until the night when moon
is mooding blue again and stars cast
shadows like violet violations
of all the lore we've come to understand.

FOR OTTO

Side by side on Father's
wide piano stool they sat,
crossing hands to grab
each other's keys –
crotchets, quavers
ricocheting the night
away in post-war
pacificity;

Dad and Otto,
his pub-found friend,
ex-POW from Camp 186
– alchemists making jazz
across the lines,
putting war to peace:
sergeants both who fought
for lands they loved.

ON WITH THE MOTLEY

When we first met you were wearing banded
Mott the Hoople socks like all young dudes
and twirling down the street to glam rock beat
of Steve Harley singing 'Make me smi-ile'.

We held hands and walked the whoopsie-do
– and now look at you, standing there bewigged,
defeminised, berating witnesses
in your courtly clothes of black and white,
consigning other people's muddled lives
to pink-tied bundled words of evidence.

When your prosecution's done, do put on
the glam, come up and see me, make me smile.

Again.

CENTURION

The hand that skims the stone is not my own
as I stand and watch by Dinas Lake,
and why the shadow when there is no sun?

Across the other side was once a camp
where Romans tried to tame the wild of Wales
and, alone, a dreaming sentry skimmed a stone.

Melting ice sheets rub and squeak on rock
as wind shoals eeling ripples underneath
– but why the shadow when there is no sun?

Centurion, your mind was home in Rome
with warmth and grapes – not frozen winterland,
downing spear to skim a foreign stone.

Puzzle shapes no longer fit as breeze-blown
corrugations drive the thaw along,
but why the shadow when there is no sun?

And here I am, two thousand years along,
watching still by Snowdon's bitten brow;
the hand that skims the stone is not my own
– and why the shadow when there is no sun?

TRAMP-LEAN

It was the way he slept, with one hand
pointing heavenwards, that caught the eye
– not so much the man with warm skull face
who slumbered on with empty bottle
by his boney side that angled on the seat;

No, it was how he leant with such content
– 'tramp-lean' would make a handy title
to the picture as a work of art –
and in that sleep what dreams might come?
Perfection in another place
denied to him by paltry circumstance?

I watched him for a while and then became
concerned lest he should be no more alive,
'til he startled up in flailing agitation
sending bottle rolling down the street
– his accusing finger pointing after it.

ILL MET BY SUNLIGHT

FISHFALL

The rod man treads dainty by the river,
a shadow chasing fishfall in the night;
he knows not where he'll cast his baited hook
until he hears circumnutating plop,
ripples purged of all baroque, as trout from sea
sucks in a fly off gliding surface skim;
it's there, in moonsplash, that he'll wait until
the water parts again and he can guess
at grub he'll match with pattern tied by him;
and so it is, in life, when we do seek
that hidden chance of catching happiness.

YOU'RE NEVER ALONE WITH A SPIDER

I call her Ida,
my six-legged spider;
you see, I checked her out
in my arachnid book
and know she's of the fairer sex;
but how she lost two
shapely legs she cannot tell.

With four one side and two
the other, she cuts a dashing
curve across the floor and ends
up near her starting point,
where she waits awhile
to regain strength for yet
another paralympic scurry.

Thinking it's the bathroom
that she wants – and a sip
of water from the tub –
I place a saucer within
six paces of her
reluctant-insect form and wait.

Two hours later she's still
standing there, and the saucer's dry.

Did she take a lick
while I wasn't looking?
Or did the water

Ill Met by Sunlight

just evaporate?
Like with the missing
legs, I'll never know for sure
– but this is what I think
about her accident:

One giant step it took
to pin my spider to the floor,
but she gamely struggled
free, losing two limbs
above the hairy knee.
Little wonder, then,
that she's reluctant
to court more danger
from this human stranger.

Each day I find her
in the room, I count
my blessings – and hers too,
and yearn to see her grow
another pair;
but she's no regenerating
worm and, besides,
I wouldn't know her then.

So I speak to her
and hope that little
by little my Ida
will learn a spider
trust of me;
my voice, her silence,
what a perfect combination!

ODE TO AN OLD ROSE

All dead roses should be dyed;
what do you think now,
what will you think then?

Just look: perplexed petals
drooling off the stem;
gone is the corolla
of concupiscence,
once pinkly deliquescent
now darkly dehydrated,
shuddering at the caress of rain.

But if you try to represent
this indignity of fading life,
you find in each charred line
and deeply darkened shade
a noble belligerence
which shimmers with a sense
of what has gone before.

So look down the stem
and see again another rose
still closed on beauty yet to come.

NO PARALLAX

I see, in parallax, a finning fish
and know he's not quite where my mind perceives
his place to be;
so is it when your wanton words conceal
the truth from me;
mostly the expression on your face tells
the story that you seek to obfuscate;
but still, in love,
I choose to take the far-fetched message
that you formulate
– believing it, the wide-eyed way, like
a bornly child startled by the life-light.

STARS ARE FALLING DOWN

Shooting stars are falling on the mountain,
dropping just before the blush of dawn
– so the shepherd says;
and as the day draws on, downcast curlew
calls across the crag, flagging rain to come.

Along the cliffs, acrobatic choughs,
in tumbling flash of red and black, pretend
to clumsiness of flight
– watched by leaping goats, not to be outdone
in their display of ledge-hop derring-do.

All these things he sees, one man and his dog
leading scattered sheep to less sparse grass
sheltered from the wind;
he knows each one of them and sheds a tear
if fluke or adder bite should take its toll.

In time of halcyon he identifies
the butterflies and flowers and curling ferns
that hide in modesty;
but tadpole spawn that dollops in the wet,
he thinks, is rot of meteorites that fall

down in the night – for how can frogs leap up
a wild Welsh peak to join his bleating sheep?
No, the word is out:

shooting stars are falling on the mountain,
dropping just before the blush of dawn.

In Wales, frogspawn on a mountain is called pydru ser
– rot of the stars.

GONE BUT NOT FORGOT

I knew you once and now you're species dead
– crossed off the list of Linnaeus, named
in Latin by lepidopterists
who marvelled at your exotic life.

Large Blue your name in English, scarce enough
when as a boy I took you in my net
– just to see your rarity, brightest
butterfly where colour matched the sky.

And then I let you go and watched you fly
into the summer sun, not knowing then
how odd your life began – caterpillar
feeding on the buds of thyme, then grabbed

by stinging ants and drawn down into
hummock nest beneath, and there your segment
gland of sweetness milked by teeming brood
who gave you food of tiny, squirming grub.

Pupating, one year on, you hatched to be
the handsome butterfly I used to see –
before you came to be extinct, now pinned
and labelled in that cabinet of time.

The Large Blue butterfly became extinct in 1979.

CAMBODIAN SMILE

Dawn light elongates the sky,
stretching pink like fingers
of a Cambodian smile –
Rodin reeling from the canvas
in swizzle-dance of line
that stirs the world to life again.

I remember this so well
because you were there to share
the moment when we woke,
reaching out to hold it
in the window frame of time,
laughing at our nakedness.

But now that you have gone,
the bluster-clouds that Turner
drew so dauntingly blot out
the bright – and grim the day
as I try to wrench you
from my mocking memory.

CRITH OF A HERON

In that warm follicle of a moment,
bent in stillness of her essence, she waits
– for ever if she must – to pounce;
zig-zagged in that awful ticking roundelay,
standing ready to detect every
little movement within her chosen
stream of consciousness – integral unzipped,
yet zipped upon itself; argal to act,
she rehearses inwardly, as turmoil
licks the arching tuck. It is the crith.

Chance will only come the once – take it;
entriggered by her mounting hunger,
she cannot miss that moment of release;
to be, to act – to act, to be, there is
no other way for bankside heron
to pass the day: assume that striking pose,
seize the moment – Prometheus unbound
yet bound to re-begin, endlessly;
when the moment's here, beak is but a spear
and finning fish have everything to fear.

All this I know as I was there, watching
too – unseen, unbeknownst to stock-still bird;
for two hours plus we were bound together
by the rushy rhythm of our river;
such steady concentration made me one

with flowing water – to act, to be,
to be, to act – until, eventually,
I barely saw the flash, the straightened zed
of neck, as spotted trout was deftly spiked
and carried off in clumsy climbing flight.

SILVER ADDER

Coiled fatly on a rock,
the adder sucked in strength
from the body-heating sun
and made ready for the hunt.

Its squat, arrow head
hid folding fangs,
ready primed with searing
yellow sting – enough
to stop a rabbit dead.

The only movement came
from its deeply-forked
black tongue as it
licked the scent of prey
from off the mountain air.

Along its stubby length
a dark zig-zag
announced its
viperous identity.

Meanwhile, a buzzard circled overhead ...

The snake, a silver
mutant, not the usual
bracken-brown, melded
in so well with its
grey bog habitat.

Ill Met by Sunlight

And on the other side of the rock ...

A young boy sat near,
unaware,
as he listened
for the noise that brought
him to the heather
hummock by the rock.

Soon it came, a distant hum
that rent the sky,
increasing in intensity
as vibrations shook
the dry cracked earth.

The adder couldn't hear
the deafening drone,
but felt the thrumming sound;
slowly, it lifted its brutal
head, swaying side to side
as its tongue tasted air.

Coiled tightly now,
it sensed the smell
of prey; but still
its coral-black eyes
could not find the target,
hidden by a tussock hump.

The boy looked up
and saw the aeroplane
– Flying Fortress, four
engines (reciting to himself),

B-17, crew of ten,
nine-bomb capacity.

Behind the bomber came
seven more, but that
was all (four missing,
thought the boy) .

His sadness grew
as the planes flew on;
and then he saw
a fluttering sheen of silver
as tiny strips of radar-fooling
screen cascaded down to him.

One fell upon the adder's
rock and the boy
reached out in search of it.

His cry of pain
was drowned
by the sound
of the last returning plane.

And as the striking adder
crawled away,
the circling buzzard
swooped on the spent, fat snake
and soared aloft
with its poisoner prey.

The boy, trying not to cry,
staggered down the hill,

clutching his swelling
hand which still held
the silver from the sky.

MOONTRAP

Gleam draws me to Tumble Mount
where a drizzle moon is caged
by careless trunks of trees –
and twilight owl soft-comforts
me with rhythm of its call.

Passing through the living bars,
I join the bright the other side
and watch stretched white wings
slide away like a dipping,
disappointed children's kite.

Bared now to interviewing
light, shouting thoughts are locked
into my head – until
a passing cloud unshackles me
and I dandy down the hill.

Darkness re-envelops me.

RELEASE

Finger twitch on fisted rein
sends a signal to the brain
of forward-reaching horse,
anticipating moment
of release from clip-clop gait
– and then she's off, beating back
the ground, daring nuzzled air
to hold her down again.

I think I know that moment now
– it was in the song we sang
together at the end,
blending bleeding hearts in such
a way that we found freedom
from each one – without descent
to music of a minor key
or words that had us hanging on.

And now we meet once more
to trot along a road the same
– and wonder who will break
the rhythm, so sedate,
we choose to hide the will
to make that great escape
from constraining ways that dull
our urge to nudge the air.

HAIKU TOO FAR

We met in some far-off bar,
a glance and double-take;
her eastern grace said *haiku*
and I configured clever
dialogue while ceremonies
of tea came to mind – she seemed
that kind of girl, serene
like snow-capped mountain or gentle

waves beneath a clenched-up sky;
and when I spoke, she said,
'You sound like a poet.
I feel uncomfortable
with that.' I gulped down the verse
and took my leave before
my napkin origami
made her really mad at me.

BYE-BYE BLUES

This is music
of what might be
– your voice cajoling me,
caught breath
and then a shout,
laughing unselfconsciously
as we spank the sand
with sock-freed feet
and race towards the sea.

You lash the waves
and gasp
at their ice caress
while our legs
are lightened
by the undertow.

But this is as far
as I can get
as I try to conjure you,
watching that slide
towards the curtain,
grateful that the image
still splashes on my mind.
Brothers we, parted
so unexpectedly.

BREATH OF BECHET

*– listening at home to Sidney Bechet's soprano
saxophone while the wind plays out a storm.*

Leaves that fall before their time,
like beech upended by a storm
and mourned as much by nature
as by man in whispered gather
of the light expanding,
while howl of wind in spaces left
changes frequency until
new growth comes to fill the gaps:

I think of this while listening
to the cadence of the notes
you blew in skitter-scatter
testament to grief and love
and downright sauciness –
trills and thrills of saxophone
describing reds and yellows,
greens and that inevitable blue;

Adulterous quavers queuing up
to crawl across the crotchets,
spanking out extended screech
of mournful semibreve, turning day
into a contradictory
night of passionate embrace;

Ill Met by Sunlight

in another time my mood
may see it differently!

But when you blew you must have thought
of places where you'd been
and people met or seen in streets
you walked or pictured in a dream
– not of nature's storms like me,
bounded by my own perceptions
in a life so far removed
from jazzy jocularities.

Petite Fleur bleeds from Bechet's sax
as storm outside runs short of breath.

RAGTIME COWBOY

Pract-is-ing trombone,
I draw an audience
of sixty cows, munching
mournful as they eyeball
me in black and white despair;

Brown Eyes Why Are You
So Blue? I play to them,
blowing against the wind
as Autumn Leaves
swirl around my head;

But Hall of the Mountain King
stampedes them into stomp
as Ellington's Morning Song
powers along, *prestissimo*,
in piston-pumping jounce of slide;

It is my Ukelele Lady
that brings them
flouncing back again
– Black Bottom swaying
the Swipsy Cakewalk way;

Mooch and My Very Good Friend
the Milkman hold them close to me
– until two bulls appear

with eyes that Blaze Away,
matching voltage of restraining wire;

Growling now, *rallentando*, I back off,
performance in the tailgate
mode, Dippermouth no match
for Bullhorn Rag – time
to beat retreat with Bye Bye Blues.

Pianissimo.

THE BOOKS THAT FELL ON ME

Sitting stocious on the floor,
I start to turn the pages
of the books that fell on me
when I embraced the shelves
in drunken search
of stimulating company.

First up, words whizzing round my head,
is *Avalanche Awareness*
by instructor Martin Epp
with whom I skied
off-piste from Andermatt
to Zermatt in a week.

It is full of bold advice:
'Like a bottle, roll your way
from out the snow sideways.'
This I do, probing as I go
to find other books
piled at foot of kitchen wall.

Jazz by Humphrey Lyttleton
has this to say to me:
'Blow your riff from memory.'
Words are floating now,
cascades of black and white
blueing music through the night.

Seamus Heaney's squat pen writes
to me, *Death of a Naturalist*
pinning down my *British Birds*
and *Fishes of the Mountain
Lakes* – and Holy Bible shalt-nots
ringing in my ears, reading

taste all very catholic
(but not to blame it
on the pub alone);
now I shift my weight
and a last book falls
– *Under Milk Wood* – on my head.

LONG-TAILED TIT

In my jumble thicket
of a hedge – blackthorn,
bramble, mint and bay –
I spied a ball of moss
and spider web with feathers
sticking out and knew
a long-tailed tit had come
to build its nest with me.

A stick on frame of quarter ounce,
tiniest of that family,
with subtle pink of rump
that puts in mind the blush
of daunting Mrs Dalloway
as she descends the stairs.
Tzee-tzee-tzee, it sings
as it binds the dome in place.

But watching all the while,
another bird of black and white
with elongated tail;
the scene is set for tragedy
as magpie swoops and leaves
a curling feather cloud
to filter down through
blood-stained mint and bay.

TURN AND TURNABOUT

His thoughts are like ripples
on the surface of a chucked-stone pond
– you can see them on his wrinkled brow.
What's he got to worry about?
Hasn't he seen another's death before?
But this is different, circumstance
is just that – his turn has come around.

The hood is pulled down on his head
by someone else who should be dead;
but war's a funny thing, they say.
He keeps on looking in his mind,
sees only that last image of the sky
– and waits for drop and rending tug,
the chance to kick out at the air.

YOU AGAIN!

I glance at you and cross
that unsafe bridge of thoughts
half-kindled – and a flame
of recognition drags
me to the other side
of memory; but where
have I seen that face before?
Not in my dreams, surely?

Suddenly a tune strikes up
and I'm dancing in the dark
at some long-forgotten
hothouse rave with moonlight
sieving through the foliage,
leopard-spotting scattered
clothes – so casually
abandoned in the trees.

And I well remember then
the music that was playing
– it was Sinatra singing
I've Got You Under My Skin –
and you were blaming me
for missing your last train
and asking when we would
be meeting once again.

OFF-BEAT

My teacher used a knuckle stick
when I practised on piano;
no thumbing of the black notes,
if you please, unless you want
another tap, she'd say to me
while the metronome clacked time.

Scales, arpeggios and chords
were just staccato smacks
and I looked forward to duets
when prod was not in reach
and fingering was all my own
while the metronome clacked time.

Counting beats was difficult
with that interfering sound;
it was the music sheet
and only what was in my head
that led to pleasant cadences
– not the metronome that clacked time.

Now the brash of jazz has taught
me how to listen while others
play that cacophony
of sound barred from me by tutting
rule of thumb – and clacking
metronome of ordered time.

THE LIE DIRECT

a politician is an arse upon
which everyone has sat

EE Cummings

Going forward! Oh, how we shudder
when we hear that redundancy
of words, the politician's
haughty disposition of dummy troops
where simple use of future tense
is for the birds and smacks too much
of truthfulness, commitment just too far

for those endowed with antic power
by hopeful vote of crushed communities;
no, call a spade a spade, square with us,
step up to the plate and democracy
will make a welcome comeback and oust
the lie direct in favour of the puff
peculiar, breath-fresh air – not hot.

Speak less, say more – wear words like a choke.

AN EVENING WITH COURTNEY PINE

Jazz night has us reaching out and waving,
bumping fists with Courtney Pine, his big fat
yulping sax in revolution mode,
a far-off cry from Way Down Yonder
in New Orleans and Rampart Street Parade
– staccato tongue licking off the quavers
like a Bren on rapid fire, rat-a-tat
crescendoing in breathless bomb-raid
siren wail, triumphal merriment of song
freed from gravitas of earthbound gravity,
streeling black notes oiled with tears of joy
as tunes familiar peel out from long improvs
of sounding pipe, hot toast melodies
dandied up in new identities
to keep the A Train running on its rails;
old ones, new ones, borrowed ones, blue
ones – no mood escapes the magic reedman's
Ali Baba thievings once the genie's out.

ILL MET BY SUNLIGHT

A plane lampoons the freshly-painted
landscape, leaving torn-cloud contrail
and turbo-jet excrescences – graffiti
scrawl across millennia of time.
She looks at me, expectantly, and speaks.

I cannot hear her voice above the jet's
ripped-curtain noise; a lapwing lollops through
the foreground sky as she talks on, questioning:
'Haven't we met somewhere?' (Screwing up her eyes
against the sun.) Now this is *my* chat-up

line – it's never been this way before.
A compliment should follow. 'I'd know that face
anywhere. You look fed-up, lonely.'
Not quite my style but not bad either.
Some interest, some concern. Me? My way

is one part kindness, two parts lust. 'I walk
this way with my dog each day. I've not seen
you here before.' The plane has vanished,
we're now alone with only earthbound sound
of our own voices. But I haven't

spoken yet – which is unusual for me.
She goes on: 'I like the solitude
and now you've broken it, you're trespassing

– but that's all right. I *do* know you, I saw
you on stage once.' She's going to ask me

for my autograph. That will be a first!
I fumble for my pen. 'You weren't very
good. You must have been having an off night.'
The dog pulls at the lead and she walks on.
Never mind the jet – I am *her* graffiti.

PASSING

How much longer
is my life?
A brief night ...

Masaoka Shiki

His dry laugh ticks in tribute
to death's mud song – and he is gone,
a blade that cut with rough-edged
sword a swathe through life he owned.

Remember days that lasted
way beyond the shine of sun?
And night-time lit by jinx as high
as merriment could guy?

Leavings of the much-loved man
are not wasted on lives of fun
– devilish doings of children's
sons and daughters yet to come.

MOUNTAIN GREENERY

Chasing mountain peak, I cross the path
of bladder fern and rock stonecrop,
then saxifrage and fir clubmoss
bring me on to base of scree, butter-pat
lines of long-healed scars, so swiftly drawn
by artist's pen, scrubbed now by light
of effervescent early morning sun;
then on and up the higher hang,
back-and-footing through a broken crack
that widens to an easy chimney stack;
mantel-shelfing now to ledge eyed from below –
and finding there, lurking luscious in the shade,
a precious little Snowdon lily flower
with leaves a sheen of green so rarely seen
at altitude – not even in a dream.

ON STATE STREET

Bejesus-bearded,
unmiraculously dressed,
he played his saxophone
– tapping out of time
with lives of passers-by
who couldn't give a toss.

And you should've heard him rant!
Between the tipple and the sax
he dealt a ditch of words
for anyone who'd listen,
claiming he'd hit the bottom
dollar – times were hard as dimes.

But pride had never left his eyes
which sparkled blue as sky,
while rain began to fill
his wishing well – making
islands of the coins
so grudgingly thrown in.

With heart he played – and not
a little soul, and when he reached
crescendo of the set
with Royal Garden Blues,
pedestrians were forced
to stop and turn and chuck

their paper money in;
then his grin was like the sun
had come to shine on him
– he'd buy himself another
lushy glug and give them
Tishomingo Rag again.

OH, DIDN'T JELLY ROLL!

Chuck in a bit
of Spanish like
a tango jerks
its rhythm beat
encountering
a step in turn
away from you
and there's the jazz
that Jelly rolled
bewitchingly
in black and white:
four dot-crotchets
to the thumping
bar biff the blues
that Morton way.
Lesser music
men hated his
pomposity –
but when he played
he proved to them
he was the best,
performance fine
exacts its fee:
a boast that 'jazz
began with me'.

GO WITH THE FLOW

Come, lean with me across this bridge,
see the river run from left to right
– weed flexing in the flow, just hanging on;
hear the music of the water, tuned
by pebble-shift and slanting of a rock,
and know, no doubt, that frequency will shape
with flood or drought as brightness, whiteness
interchange with shadows cast by sun;
hope for glimpse of fish, speckled grace of trout
finning in and out of places hidden
from the light; dream your thoughts away
downstream, knowing they will never come
to you again on this ancient arch of stone.

NIGHT LIFE

The nightjar swoops and yaws
and churrs its song, cracks
its white-blobbed wings
in little echoes off the *clog*
that rears from moorland heath;

Dusk has come and insects
rising from the sun-warmed
ground are targeted
relentlessly in waddle
airborne frenzy feed;

Attracted by its signal
flight, a drabber, mottled
mate with bristle gape
joins the 'jar in Morfa
Bychan's fading light;

Below, an adder winds
between the bracken stems
in secret stalk of pulsing
prey that will not live
to see another day;

While, steep above them all,
a kestrel hovers
with the same intent;

higher still, a silver streak
tears a crevice in the sky;

Night descends on land
once occupied by sea –
and mountains to the north
and east of Wales
vanish in the purple gloom.

THE HARE THAT DIPPED ITS PAWS

The hare that dipped its paws
was on the beach each day,
bathing in the suck-back
suckle of the surf.

It might have been a child
at paddle-play and seemed
to love the sun that dried
its prints into the sand.

Joining it one time
were its leverets
– offspring out to share
the healing seaside fun.

Last day I visited
the shore, the young
were there alone – searching
through the gentle waves.

THAT PURE THING

Leavened by the lilt of language,
unkindest thoughts are rendered
in baroque – prettied up
with rococo dialect,
wrapped in charm of purplement;

My missive is a lie
and you always fall for it
as I smile the scowl away;

Would you prefer it then
delivered unadorned,
jagged by sharp sincerity
– red clinker glow fanned
by breath of molten moment?

Better let me save you
from myself that we may lick
away the bitterness;

But just you do the same
and we can share this nicety;
with love the message
is the mind – and we
dare not prevaricate;

Rossetti's Wombat

For who wants speech adorned
with swanking plumes of fluff,
arras that fails to hide the truth?

It is you whose vision kills
with precision stab
the part of me that hides
the hurt; now we clear the decks,
speak plain, live again;

So our new cogs mesh
and lubricated wheels
turn in perfect harmony;

For we've built a room inside
our cluttered living space
where no proud furniture
can detract from what we share:
that pure thing we call love.